Mark Briegal is a founding partner at Bennett Briegal LLP, a specialist legal practice advising other lawyers and professionals on the business of law, partnership matters, mergers and acquisitions, business structures, professional regulation and employment.

Mark was on the Executive Board of a Top 200 law firm during a period of sustained growth. He originally worked in banking, running a range of banking operations for Chase Manhattan Bank, and then in management consulting, before qualifying as a solicitor. Mark aims to bring a very practical approach to business law.

Mark has an MBA from Manchester Business School and a Classics degree from Cambridge University. He took the PgDL and LPC at the College of Law in Chester.

Mark set up Association of Partnership Practitioners in the North West and now sits on its committee. He has been ranked in Legal 500 and Chambers legal directories.

Mark has advised solicitors, doctors, dentists, accountants, haulage contractors, farmers and a range of other professionals on all aspects of their partnerships and LLPs. He also advises professionals who are incorporated into limited companies.

Mark deals with the creation of partnerships and LLPs, the exit of partners, whether by retirement or expulsion, the conversion of partnerships and sole traders to LLPs and the dissolution or incorporation into limited companies of partnerships and LLPs.

With a pragmatic approach, he acts for both the continuing partners and for those exiting the partnership or LLP in a range of disputes. His aim is to resolve the dispute as quickly and painlessly as possible whilst getting the best deal for his clients.

Mark has extensive experience of mergers and acquisitions in the professional partnership sector and has advised on a number of law firm and accountancy mergers.

Additionally, as an experienced and well-regarded presenter, Marks regularly speaks on all aspects of partnership and commercial law. He has presented at Manchester Business School, the University of Law, the Lexis Nexis Partnership Conference, The Law Society, MBL Seminars, Chester University and UKTI, as well as designing and teaching on the legal module on the University of Glyndŵr MBA programme.

Outside of work, Mark is involved in sports. He is currently Chair of Archery GB, the national governing body for Archery in the UK and, as a former quite-competitive rower, is now a qualified rowing coach and multi-lane endorsed umpire. He chairs the British Rowing North West Umpire Committee. He is also a Trustee of the Rowing Foundation, a charity which promotes the participation in rowing of young people and the disabled of all ages.

Mark is married with adult children (and a cat) and lives in Cheshire. Trips to the gym counter Mark's love of food and wine. Travel also features where possible.

Mark can be contacted on mark@bennettbriegal.co.uk or 07973 283678.

A Concise Guide to Solving Partnership and LLP Disputes Without Litigation

A Concise Guide to Solving Partnership and LLP Disputes Without Litigation

Mark Briegal MA (Cantab) MBA

Law Brief Publishing

Published 2021 by Law Brief Publishing, an imprint of Law Brief Publishing Ltd
30 The Parks
Minehead
Somerset
TA24 8BT

www.lawbriefpublishing.com

Paperback: 978-1-913715-69-4

ACKNOWLEDGEMENTS

Any errors are my fault.

I'd like to thank all those who have supported, encouraged and challenged me on my journey through partnership law. That includes both the great lawyers I have had the privilege to work with and many I have had the challenge of working against, most of whom have done so politely and professionally with no personal animosity, as we appreciate that each is doing his or her best for their client.

My business partner Paul Bennett is a tower of support and has encouraged me through the process of writing a book, having been there himself. I often call on his tactical genius when solving partnership disputes. He also makes me laugh.

Tim Kevan at Law Brief Publishing has been an invaluable editor.

@partnershipcat (please follow her on Twitter) has been of little use, but is a good companion when she's in the mood.

Finally, and most importantly, my wife Clare has as ever been very supportive and understanding as I embark upon yet another "good idea".

Mark Briegal
September 2021

CONTENTS

CHAPTER ONE

INTRODUCTION

If you are looking for a book on partnership or LLP law, you are reading the wrong book.

There are plenty of excellent books on black letter partnership and LLP law, such as the iconic Lindley & Banks on Partnership and Whittaker and Machell's Law of Limited Liability Partnerships.

The aim of this book is to pick up on many years' experience of dealing with partnership disputes at a practical level, mainly in the professional sector, and resolving disputes without recourse to litigation or arbitration.

This book is mainly aimed at dealing with professional practice disputes, although a partnership is a partnership and the same range of outcomes is possible whether you are dealing with solicitors or haulage contractors. A farmer I once advised on a very messy dispute with his partner listened politely to my advice, thanked me for my time and said he was going to "go round there with a baseball bat" instead. That is of course strongly not advised, and - more importantly - should be unnecessary.

In this short and practical book, we'll be looking at why disputes arise and the key elements involved in settling them. Most professionals realise that a long and protracted dispute benefits no-one apart from the lawyers. Additionally, many do not want to wash their proverbial dirty linen in public as that is not good for professional reputations; either for the firm or the partner.

Most partnership disputes follow a fairly well-worn path and this book aims to help the reader navigate that path and deal with the occasional curve ball that comes their way.

This book is based on the Law in England and Wales as at 31st July 2021.

A note on terminology

In this book, I will use the word "partner" to denote a partner in a true 1890 Partnership Act general partnership, a member or an LLP or even a director/shareholder in a limited company, unless it is relevant to be more precise. Similarly, I'll use the word "firm" to denote the partnership, LLP or company concerned, unless the difference is relevant.

As we will see in Chapter 3, the difference is crucial in terms of the routes to the end, but the word partner works well to describe an individual with a stake in a professional firm.

CHAPTER TWO

WHY PARTNERSHIP DISPUTES ARISE

Many years ago I advised some professionals on buying a practice together. The costs of buying a practice are never low and the final piece of the jigsaw in my advice was that they needed a partnership agreement. They decided that they had spent enough money and besides, they were old school friends and had known each other for years, so what could possibly go wrong?

This next paragraph is probably unnecessary. You will have guessed that all was not sweetness and light in their partnership and the saved £1,000 or so on a partnership agreement was replaced by tens of thousands of pounds of legal costs in a very messy partnership dispute. Their professional regulator was unimpressed by the fist fight in reception.

This was a scenario that even the best drafted of partnership agreements would not necessarily have solved. It would of course have provided a simpler and cheaper process for resolving the underlying dispute.

Early Discussions

The best time to avoid a partnership dispute is when you're getting on. In the honeymoon stages of a business relationship, when you are setting up the business, it makes sense to have the difficult conversations because they are all hypothetical. We are not going to fall out, but if we did how would we resolve it?

Once I have drafted a partnership or LLP agreement for a professional practice, my advice is always to lock it in a drawer and leave it there gathering dust. The minute anyone is tempted to take it out from the drawer and see what it says, then there is a potential partnership dispute brewing.

At that point, it is best to leave the drawer locked and go to the pub or coffee shop (or wherever) and to have a frank and possibly difficult conversation. Get to the bottom of the issues and decide what you're going to do about it. Record what you've decided and move on.

Once you start checking what the partnership agreement says, you are possibly at the top of a potentially slippery slope.

The Agreement

As you will have seen from the paragraph above, a well drafted partnership or LLP agreement is the basis for avoiding disputes. Those early discussions setting out what happens in what situations are key.

I remember my history tutor at university stating that the key to understanding ancient history was to remember "land, money, power." In many respects, that is equally the case in partnership disputes. Land is probably less important, but money and power are the key drivers in partnership disputes.

The two major areas of dispute that arise within partnerships are around profit sharing and decision-making. Who gets how much of the profits and who gets to take the important decisions? If you can resolve those two matters, then a partnership dispute is unlikely to arise. Hence the need to have honest discussions early on and to tackle issues when they arise or even when they might arise.

The key elements that need to go into a good Partnership or LLP Agreement, and which can cause friction are:

- Capital – how much is the partner required to put in and when. Are there situations when additional capital will be required and what happens if a partner cannot afford or does not wish to put more capital into the firm? How and when will that capital be returned? See below on retirement.

- Profits and losses -how will they be divided? This can run on a continuum from equality to "eat what you kill". In equality, the profits are divided equally between the partners, irrespective of how much effort or success (however you define success) each one has put in or achieved. At the other end of the spectrum, "eat what you kill" sees partners taking only that share of profits which they have generated, billed and – hopefully – collected. Yet another argument can arise around how expenses are allocated in this scenario. Some partners share an administrative assistant, and others demand their own, and possibly more than one! And certain partners demand a lot more central support than others.

There are many options in the middle of this continuum. I personally like a partner's profit share to have an element reflecting the salary due to them for the work that they do as a senior professional, a performance related element based on how they have performed against an agreed set of SMART[1] objectives and a final dividend element based on their capital, to reflect their investment in the firm. Without a clear definition, which may include an element of give-and-take for good and bad years, or an averaging calculation, resentment can arise. Those contributing more to the firm can resent those contributing less. Similar discussions can be had regarding losses, although note that it is best practice to allocate losses in an LLP into a Loss Reserve Account, where they remain in the LLP until needed for tax purposes.

- Drawings Policy – who gets to take out how much and when? Again, if this is not agreed, disputes can easily arise. It is usual to agree a monthly draw so that partners know that they can pay their mortgages and monthly bills. Addition profit shares can then be taken as agreed, often after the annual accounts have been finalised and the profits agreed. Some firms have additional draws quarterly or semi-annually.

- Decision making – who gets to make what decisions? Is there a management committee to whom powers have been delegated or is it by a simple or weighted majority? If so, is it a majority based purely on numbers, or by percentage of capital or points? Are there tiers of partner with different voting rights? All partners need to understand how decisions will be made. The 2021 case of Tribe v Elborne Mitchell LLP the judge found that he allocation of profit had been

---

[1] Specific, Measurable, Achievable, Relevant and Timebound.

'within the range of proposals that it was reasonable for the senior partner to make'. What is in the Partnership of LLP Agreement will stand unless it is perverse.

It is good practice, wherever possible, to avoid taking votes on matters at partners' meetings. The minute you take a vote, there is somebody who has "lost" and who may feel resentful at that decision. It is preferable, if it is clear that there is a minority strongly against a particular decision, to adjourn the meeting and for a senior partner to try to resolve the issue before bringing it back to the table, or to reach a compromise. If you have to take a vote leaving a minority disgruntled, careful management will be required to ensure that this does not turn into a full blown dispute.

- Retirement and expulsion – it needs to be clear how these clauses work and partners need to feel that they cannot be unfairly ganged-up on and forced out. The majority of partners need a mechanism to deal with poorly performing partners. The mechanisms need to be appropriate to the size and culture of the firm. In a large firm with a corporate culture, the mechanism can be quite brutal. If the management committee decides that partner A is to retire, partner A will retire. In a firm with five or fewer partners, such a brutal mechanism will not be appropriate, but nonetheless the firm needs a mechanism to deal with poor performance or, more likely, poor behaviours.

There is usually a debate about whether an agreement should have a no-fault expulsion clause. We often call this a "red socks clause" because it allows the partners to remove a partner because he or she wears red socks. The issue with fault expulsion clauses is that the non-performing partner's performance or behaviour is not quite bad enough to force a fault expulsion, but there is a general acknowledgement in the firm that it would be a better place without him or her. I mention above performance or behaviour, and in my experience it is often the behaviour that is the issue.

If your agreement contains a well drafted no-fault expulsion clause, you probably don't need to read further!

- Restrictive covenants – again you can go off and read many learned tomes on the tricky subject of restrictive covenants. The key in partnership disputes is to have them as a negotiating tool; partners need to appreciate what they can and cannot do. As we will see later, they can be a vital negotiation tool as a partner may be desperate to take some of his or her clients with them.

- Dispute resolution – you need to decide whether or not your partnership agreement has either mediation and or arbitration in it. There are pros and cons to both. When it comes to a dispute, it is vital to know whether mediation and arbitration is in the partnership agreement and whether it prohibits the disgruntled partner, or the firm, from starting a claim before going through the alternative dispute procedures.

- It is useful, especially in larger firms where there is a management committee, to have a clause in the agreement that allows that management committee to take legal advice in the event of a dispute, which can be paid for by the by the firm and – crucially – cannot be seen by the partner whose potential removal or sanction is being contemplated. Without such a clause, there is a risk that a partner can claim access to all documents and advice provided to the firm. If such a clause is not in the agreement, it is safer for the individual partners to take advice in their own names. They will not be able to claim back the VAT on this.

Tackle issues

For some reason, it is not uncommon for partners in professional practices not to want to tackle poor performers, be that in terms of billing, technical competence or interpersonal behaviours. This may be because people get to become partners in firms because they are technically competent at accountancy, law, surveying, medicine, etc and then are expected to manage a team, generate business and run a practice – all of which are skills they have never been taught. Additionally, people (even aggressive litigators) often do not like confrontation with people close to them on a face to face basis.

The ostrich approach to management never yields good results. A problem ignored does not improve. In fact, a problem tackled may well improve. A recently promoted partner, new in the role, who is taken aside by a trusted more senior and experienced partner, may well listen to advice and change their ways before their behaviour becomes so destructive that they are asked to leave.

Trying to persuade a head of department partner who has been in role for 20 years that he or she should alter their approach is not going to be an easy conversation, especially if they are a big biller. A well drafted partnership agreement may help, as well as good performance reviews and a well-managed HR function.

Given the issue identified above – that people are made partners because they are technically proficient at whatever the firm's specialism is, rather than because they have the appropriate skill set to manage a team, win new business and develop a firm – it is key that new partners are given a thorough induction programme to being a partner, possibly a mentor to help them develop as a partner and regular feedback to prevent them getting bad habits early on.

This must be an ongoing process and a good appraisal system is key.

Where a problem is tackled well and sensitively as soon as it arises, is less likely to lead to a fully-blown partnership dispute.

CHAPTER THREE

THE DIFFERENCE BETWEEN PARTNERSHIP AND LLP DISPUTES

If you are an experienced partnership practitioner and are comfortable that you know the differences between a general partnership under the 1890 Act and an LLP, please feel free to skip this chapter.

At the risk of stating "the bleedin' obvious", you must be very clear what entity you are dealing with. I am using the term "partner" to describe anybody with an ownership or management stake in a firm. Once you are dealing with a dispute, you need to know whether it is a dispute between partners, a dispute between a member of an LLP and that LLP, or even a dispute between members of an LLP.

Limited Companies

This is a book about partnership disputes, which also includes LLPs, because they have a lot of similarities in regards to dealing with partnership with disputes.

I am however going to devote a paragraph or two on limited companies because more and more professional firms are incorporating as limited companies, because of the potential tax advantages (at the time of going to press), but still regard themselves as a "partnership".

There are also the quasi-partnership provisions of the Companies Act that relate to small limited companies and impact on just and equitable winding up.

I have learnt the hard way very early on to stop callers who phone me to ask for "partnership" advice. They often talk about "my partner has done this" or "my partner has done that", but it becomes apparent that they are actually co-directors and shareholders in a limited company.

Much of the later aspects of this book on negotiating tactics and possible outcomes are still relevant to limited companies, especially where there are only two or three shareholders, although the settlement mechanics will be different.

The big difference is that directors in limited company firms are nearly always employees as well as officers, and are therefore covered by employment legislation.

A well drafted no fault expulsion clause in a Partnership or LLP Agreement will allow for a partner to be removed with a few consequences, so long as there is no discrimination. Such a clause is not possible within the limited company framework, as it is not possible to agree to exclude employment law.

One of the joys of LLPs versus limited companies is the flexibility that an LLP provides, especially around capital maintenance, and removing a partner is so much more straightforward as a share in a partnership or LLP includes both management and ownership, whereas in a limited company framework you have to consider the employment aspects of the director and the shares owned by the shareholder.

We have dealt recently with a number of "partnership disputes" with small limited company law firms and the time and effort in resolving them has far exceeded that usually required in a partnership or LLP dispute. There have been concurrent employment claims and minority shareholder protection claims which have increased the complexity and cost of resolving the disputes. Mediation eventually worked, but an LLP would have made life quicker, simpler and cheaper.

In terms of shareholdings, a limited company has is governed by section 994 etc of the Companies Act 2006 which provides minority shareholder protection. This cannot be ruled out in the shareholders agreement, although a valuation mechanism and a dispute resolution mechanism can be included. Note, however, that Section 994 etc can be excluded from an LLP Agreement, and usually is.

There are, as ever, pros and cons to excluding Section 994. It is usually excluded as it prevents partners from bringing actions against the LLP if they feel hard done by. If the LLP Agreement contains an arbitration clause, which is usual, then it forces any disputes into arbitration. As discussed elsewhere in this book, the advantage of an arbitration clause is that it prevents the washing of dirty linen in public. At the time of writing, it can take a long time for any dispute to come before the courts and therefore arbitration will may get a quicker result. It is not necessarily any cheaper than the court system, but may be more under the control of the parties.

The argument advanced for allowing members of an LLP to bring Section 994 proceedings against the LLP is that it may keep the

Management their powers to the disadvantage of other members. It is rare for it not to be excluded.

Partnerships v LLPs

The first obvious statement is that a partnership is not a separate entity. A partnership does not exist as an entity in itself, but is a joint endeavour between the partners. Therefore any partnership dispute is a dispute between the partners.

Conversely, an LLP is a separate entity and a dispute can arise between a member of an LLP and the LLP. Disputes can also arise between members of LLPs.

A partnership is governed by the Partnership Act 1896 whereas an LLP is governed by the LLP Act 2000, and the LLP Regulations and indirectly by the Companies Act 2006.

Good Faith

A fiduciary duty exists between partners and partnership agreements nearly always include a duty of good-faith, or even a duty of utmost good faith, between the partners.

Good faith is not implied into the relationship between an LLP and its members. An LLP agreement often includes a duty of good-faith between the members and the LLP. It is a matter of discussion as to whether or not there should be a duty between the members of an LLP. I prefer it is not there, because its absence prevents disgruntled members from taking action against other members. A duty of good-faith between the LLP and its members makes sense and a member can take action against the LLP if it has acted towards him or her not in good faith and an LLP, acting through whatever decision-making process it has agreed, can bring an action against one of its members.

An underlying theme in this book is the need to check the underlying constitutional document or documents that govern the dispute. A key point to check is whether there is a duty of good-faith written into an LLP Agreement, and whether it is between the member and the LLP or whether it also applies between the members.

A duty of good faith is a given in a partnership dispute. Clause 28 of the Partnership Act 1890 states, "Partners are bound to render true accounts and full information of all things affecting the partnership to any partner or his legal representatives.", and the case law backs it up. In the limited company scenario, directors have a fiduciary duty to their companies.

The issue of minority shareholder protection, mentioned above, is also relevant here, where the firm is set up as a limited company.

Partnerships

We have established that, in a partnership, any dispute is between the partners and is governed by the Partnership Act 1896 and the terms of any agreed Partnership Agreement. There is also an implied duty of good-faith between the partners.

Where there is a dispute between partners, it is usual to take a Partnership Account. Clause 28 of the Partnership Act allows any partner to demand details from their partners of all transactions and dealings that they been a party to in relation to the partnership. This is often used as a means to resolve intractable disputes as to money as the Court will order an Account, where the Partnership Agreement does not specify a dispute resolution mechanism.

The other potentially useful mechanism in a traditional partnership is around dissolution. The partnership act 1890 allows any partner to dissolve the partnership. Clause 32(c) says: "Subject to any agreement between the partners, a partnership is dissolved ... (c) If entered into for an undefined time, by any partner giving notice to the other or others of his intention to dissolve the partnership".

A well-drafted partnership agreement will exclude this and prevent an individual partner from dissolving the partnership, but where there is no Partnership Agreement or the Partnership Agreement is silent on the matter, the threat of dissolution can be a very powerful tool in a partnership dispute, especially where one partner is in dispute with a larger number of partners in a bigger firm, where the threat of dissolution is real and expensive.

I have, on occasions, had a partner sign a notice of dissolution and left it undated. I have sent a scanned copy of this signed but undated notice of dissolution to the other side with a note stating that we just need to date it for the partnership to be dissolved, with all that entails. Given the cost and disruption of a dissolution, It can bring parties to the negotiating table.

Note also that clause 25 says, "No majority of the partners can expel any partner unless a power to do so has been conferred by express agreement between the partners." Without a Partnership Agreement in place with a methodology of removing partners, it is not possible to remove a partner. This clause is useful for a partner where his or her partners are attempting to remove them in a situation with no agreement, as they can only be removed by negotiation or dissolution.

Please remember that dissolution is the start of the process in the partnership, whereas this is the end of the process for an LLP or limited company.

Dissolution should really be a last resort. The process of dissolution involves appointing a receiver, at cost, or the partners agreeing to cooperate, to wind up the partnership. This involves realising all the partnership's assets, paying the partnership's liabilities and sharing any surplus in accordance with Section 44 of the Partnership Act 1896.

The key thing to remember is that on notice of dissolution, the bank will almost inevitably freeze the partnership's bank accounts. Other creditors and clients/customers will lose faith and any value that was in the business, which is now – in most cases – unable to trade, will be destroyed. Hence the threat of dissolution is so powerful.

LLPs

In an LLP, the dispute should be between the LLP and its member, especially if there is a well drafted agreement.

The first thing to check is that there is no duty of good-faith between the members and what the LLP Agreement says.

An LLP without an agreement is more problematic than a partnership without an agreement as the Partnership Act has 125 years of case law to clarify what happens in a range of situations.

The LLP Act only came into force in 2002 and therefore has less than 20 years of case law. Partnership law can be useful to see what might happen in an LLP, although of course the Companies Act also applies. It can sometimes be worrying when a client asks what the case law is on a particular LLP problem, and the response from experts is, "We're not sure".

An LLP is also regulated by the Limited Liability Partnership Regulations 2001. These add a little, but not much. The key point to note from the LLP Regulations, is that clause 7 set out some default provisions for LLPs and, crucially clause 8 states, "No majority of the members can expel any member unless a power to do so has been conferred by express agreement between the members." This is the same as in a partnership; see above.

Because the LLP is more akin to a limited company than a partnership, the process of dissolution is similar to a limited company. Either the members agree to it or a court does it. There is a liquidation of the assets and then the LLP is removed from the register at Companies House.

Most LLP Agreements contain a clause requiring a high percentage of members to agree to a winding up, so it is unlikely to happen. The risks of winding up are similar to that in a partnership, so it is again a last resort solution to a partnership dispute in an LLP.

Limited Partnerships

The final type of partnership is a Limited Partnership under the Limited Partnership Act 1907. These are both rare and complex. They tend to be used predominantly for very wealthy family trusts and hedge funds. Given this, there is nearly always a constitutional document in place and any dispute is beyond the scope of this book. The general principles will always apply, but you will need very specialist advice to deal with it.

Conclusion

You need to check carefully what entity you are dealing with; whether it is a partnership, an LLP or even a limited company will determine how are you progress with the dispute.

Secondly, you need to check whether or not there is a constitutional document relating to the entity you are dealing with.

If there is no document then you are thrown back to the Companies Act and Articles of Association for a limited company, the LLP regulations for an LLP and the Partnership Act for an 1890 general partnership.

CHAPTER FOUR

DECIDING THE PARAMETERS

Introduction

This is key to settling a partnership dispute without resorting to litigation. You need to understand the parameters of the dispute that you are dealing with. This will be key to reaching a settlement. You need to understand what entity you are dealing with and what its constitutional document (if any) says, but – based on experience of dealing with hundreds, if not thousands – of partnership disputes over the last 20 years, an understanding of where they are likely to go is vital.

The usual outcomes

I am not guaranteeing that this will happen, but it is usual – especially in firms with five or more partners – that in the event of a dispute between one partner and the firm, the end result is that the one partner leaves.

If there has been a falling out then it becomes virtually impossible for that partner to remain working in the firm because of the bad feeling that has inevitably arisen during the dispute and because of whatever the underlying issues that led to the dispute initially.

Dissolution is normally an extremely poor result for all the parties and therefore, unless one side or the other has a "death-wish" and is determined to drag the other side down with them, a resolution will be reached in which the partner leaves the firm and the firm continues without him or her.

Once you have reached that conclusion, it boils down to the terms on which the partner leaves. They will usually leave with their profit share to the date of leaving, some or all of their capital, potentially some payment for goodwill, often some agreed clients and an agreed reference. We will look at all of these in more detail in the chapter on negotiation, but for the most part this is what a settlement will look like.

In a two-partner firm the usual outcome is different. There are only four possible outcomes:

1. A buys out B and B leaves

2. B buys out A and A leaves

3. The whole firm is sold to a third party

4. The firm is wound up

It can be worthwhile stating these four, and only four, outcomes to the other side to see how they react. It may be useful for them to see the stark realities that face them.

Once they realise this, it usually boils down to one of the four options being the best way forward. As discussed above, dissolution or winding up rarely produces the best outcomes for all parties, especially if the business is trading and has a value. With professional firms, especially solicitors, there is a cost to closing down and that can be high.

A sale to a third party is always a possibility, but once there is a dispute and some urgency, it looks like a "fire sale" and fire sales rarely produce best value.

That means that either of the parties should buy out the other and, in many cases, it is clear that one is more keen to continue than the other, so the outcome is obvious.

If they both want to continue, but without the other – possibly because they have different visions for the business – then there may need to be an auction of the highest price. If negotiation cannot resolve the matter, then the two most common solutions are Sealed Bids or Russian Roulette.

In Sealed Bids each party puts in an offer to an independent third party by an agreed set time and the highest offer wins, with that party obliged to buy out the other one at their bid price.

With so called Russian Roulette one party put in a bid at a price and the other party has two options – either to sell his or her share at the offered price or, conversely, to flip the offer and buy the offering party's share at the price offered. In this case the offering party has no choice but to sell at that price. The logic of this is that the party making the offer cannot bid too low as, if they do, the offer may be flipped against them and they will have to sell their share of the partnership at that price. It should make the offering party consider their options and their offer price very carefully.

A potential risk of both these strategies is that if one party has greater access to funds than the other and knows that the other will not easily be able to get the funds, they can put in a low bid knowing the other will not be able to match it or to refuse it. In such cases it is advisable to get an independent third-party valuer to value the firm. The nature of the valuer will depend on the activity if the firm. Law and accountancy firms are usually valued by accountants, whereas property firms with a portfolio are valued by RICS valuers.

The possibilities

Once you've worked this out and realised where you will eventually get to, it then boils down to the BIG question.

And the BIG question is simply: How much?

At its most simple level, partnership disputes boil down to the fact that the partner who is in dispute with the others will leave and then it is a case of deciding how much he or she will get and the payment terms involved.

This can be through detailed assessment of the firm's accounts and the terms of any partnership agreement, or through simple horse-trading. It usually involves an element of each.

Arbitration

You need to watch out for an arbitration clause in either a Partnership Agreement or an LLP Agreement. If there is an arbitration clause in your constitutional document, and it is probably there in over 50% of cases, it is open to either party in the dispute to invoke it. Once that happens, you are on a path of time and cost, although it will be quicker, and more private, than going to court.

If the other party is not entering into negotiations, or is being difficult, it can sometimes be useful to threaten arbitration to bring them to the table or to drop an objection once they realise the time and cost implications.

An arbitration clause usually involves the parties agreeing to appoint an arbitrator and, in the absence of agreement for a third party – often the President of the Law Society, the Institute of Chartered Accountants in England and Wales or one of the arbitration organisations – to appoint them, again incurring additional time and expense.

A simple email that says, "We appear to be at an impasse. Here are three potential arbitrators; do you agree to one of them being appointed?", can often result in a return to the negotiating table.

CHAPTER FIVE

NEGOTIATION

Introduction

The key to negotiation is knowing what is important to the other person.

Offering someone something that has no value to them is pointless. You want to offer them something that has value to them, and ideally something that is cheap or easy for you to provide.

Looking at partnership disputes the key areas around which negotiation usually takes place are as follows:

- How much will the leaving partner be paid?

- When will the agreed sum be paid?

- How will be sum paid be apportioned for tax?

- Who will pay their tax payments?

- How will leaving accounts be prepared?

- What indemnities will be required either way?

- Will restrictive covenants be enforced, or will there be exceptions allowed?

- What agreed statements will be made to staff, clients, the market?

- What confidentiality will be applied about the departure?

- Kit – laptops, phones, cars, etc?

- Intellectual property – precedents, etc?

We will look at each of these in turn, but before we do, let's consider negotiation in a bit more detail.

Negotiation

The aim of negotiation is to reach a settlement with the other person. It necessarily involves some give and take. Making a series of demands and offering nothing in return is not negotiation. It may work if the other side is desperate.

The style will depend on who has the strongest hand, but the skill lies in looking for the strengths in your own hand, however weak it may initially seem, and finding weaknesses in apparently strong hands.

You need to do your preparation – see below – and be prepared to offer something, but hopefully something that is easy for you to give, but is more important to the other side.

When teaching negotiation, I often start with the analogy of buying a car. You start by doing your homework. What prices are different garages or retailers offering? Is there a glut of the model you want, and therefore lots of opportunities to get a bargain, or is it in short supply, so you'll have to try harder. Is it a new model or one soon to be replaced? What time of year is it – bargains can be had before the plates change if you're prepared not to have the latest plate?

Once you get into the garage, you want to show that you're willing to buy, but not at any price and that you know the market.

The areas for negotiation listed above then come into play. Are you paying cash? Will you use their credit scheme (they get commission)? Do you have a part exchange?

What's cheap for them but worth more to you? Road tax and fuel would cost each party the same, so are not relevant to the negotiation – they are the same as a cash reduction. As a buyer, paying cash or having no part exchange may be worth more to the seller and they can throw in extras that they get at cost price and the buyer has to pay retail – sets of mats, other extras or a "free" service. It may not be free, but the cost to the garage of providing you a service is less than the cost of you buying it.

A key one of these "free but worth a lot" extras in a partnership dispute is a reference or an agreed statement. It can be worth a lot to the leaving partner if he or she is seen to be leaving on good terms, but costs the firm nothing, apart from possibly having to bite their lip a little bit. This is discussed in greater detail below.

A matter of principle

My heart tends to sink a little when I hear the phrase, "It's a matter of principle". These words often imply that the other party is not really open for negotiation, but is out to make a point, even if it ends up to their disadvantage.

I am reminded of a wily litigator who once quipped, "Oh; It's a point of principle, is it? In that case I'm willing to fight it to the very end … of your cheque book!".

You must accept that there is give and take in negotiations.

It is a truism that a good settlement often involves both parties being a bit disappointed. The departing partner always wanted a bit more and the firm always wanted to pay a bit less, but if the deal is done and the parties can move on without additional costs and time, that is a result.

It is not uncommon to settle litigation, even though you have a good chance of winning, to save costs and time. There may be moral reasons not to, but commercially it can make sense (so long as you are not setting a precedent) to pay a vexatious litigant £500, rather than spend £10,000 in legal fees and have senior managers out the organisation for serval days in court or a tribunal.

The aim must always be to get the other side into a negotiation.

How much will the leaving partner be paid?

As mentioned earlier, "how much" is often the big question in a partnership dispute.

Depending on the nature and Constitution of the partnership or LLP concerned, this may well be set out in the agreement.

The key elements that make up a payment are:

- Profit-share due to the departure date.

- Payment in lieu of notice.

- The repayment of some or all of the departing partner's capital in the business.

- What happens to any tax reserve.

- Goodwill.

- Any ex-gratia payment.

In reality, these elements are often combined and an element of "horse-trading" takes place between the partners to come up with a global figure payable on departure.

Sometimes partners will depart purely on the basis of the existing partnership or LLP agreement, but if that were the case you probably would not be reading this! In the majority of cases a separate Deed of Retirement is drawn up to amend the terms of any agreement, especially when the agreements do not reflect the agreed departure terms.

I have seen some very old partnership agreements where the departing partner is due his or her capital in full on their date of departure. Where this coincides with partners having large capital balances and the firm not having much cash, this creates a problem. In a traditional partnership the departing partner could in theory bankrupt their partners.

The profit share to departure date is not usually too controversial as the departing partner will be due it. One area to be careful on is around accounts. It is not uncommon for the continuing partners to delay billing at the end of the departing partner's final year, and to hold it off to the next year, when they are not sharing profit with the outgoing partner. Similarly costs can be brought forward to the current year, again depressing profit and then bad debt provisions can be increased, along with write offs and provisions for things never before provided for. The Deed of Retirement needs to take this into account.

The Deed of Retirement must include a mechanism for agreeing the accounts and how they are prepared. It must ensure that the accounts are produced on the same basis as previous years and any extraordinary items are agreed. There should be a mechanism of referring disputes to an independent expert.

Payment in lieu of notice is not a partnership concept; it is an employment law concept. Nonetheless it may be contractual in a partnership or LLP Agreement and if the firm wants a partner out, it may be willing to pay him or her notice to get them off the premises. If there is a garden leave clause then this may be used to stop them setting up in competition. When relationships have broken down, it often makes sense just to get the difficult person out the offices.

Capital should be discernable from the firm's accounts, but can be tricky to get right, especially if the firm does not keep separate capital and current accounts. A partner should not necessarily assume that he or she will get back all of the fixed capital they have invested in the firm. As all adverts for share offerings stare, the value of investments can go down as well as up, and an investment of capital in a partnership or LLP is no different. There has historically been an acceptance (and the matching cash) in professional partnerships that partners get their capital back when they retire, but that is not nor should be regarded as a given. Part of the negotiations will be how much of their capital a departing partner gets. If the firm as a whole is worth less than when they joined, it makes sense that their capital will have also diminished. Conversely, there is an argument that if the firm is worth more, their capital will have increased, but often partnership of LLP Agreements preclude this.

It is best to start with the presumption that, unless there is an agreement to the contrary, a partner will expect back the amount of capital he or she has paid into the business, unless there has been an obvious change to the worth of the business, especially in a downwards direction.

If the firm retains tax money to pay partners' tax (generally a good thing), there can be negotiations as to what happens to that. It is the partner's money and he or she is entitled to it, although some firms use it as cash flow. For the outgoing partner, he or she should aim to get hold of it as soon as possible, it as it is safer for them to have it in case the firm goes bust and the partner of course remains personally liable for his or her tax. This is often negotiable and depends on the financial standing of the firm.

Goodwill

This brings us to the tricky subject of goodwill. A good accountancy textbook will tell you that goodwill is the excess over the value of net assets in the purchase price. If a firm has net assets of £100 and a buyer is prepared to pay £150 for the firm, there is £50 of goodwill.

Goodwill matters because a buyer can depreciate it and get a tax saving and a partner can, if they have been a partner for two years, pay capital gains tax at 10% on any gain by claiming Business Asset Disposal (BAD) relief – which used to be called Entrepreneurs Relief (ER).

There is much debate as to whether goodwill exists in a professional firm. Where the firm exists on the traditional model where a partner pays in capital on joining, takes a share of profits during their time as a partner, and then gets their capital back on retirement, there is often little goodwill. If the firm can continue to generate good profits when the partner leaves, or if the value if the firm has increased significantly during their time as a partner, there is an argument that goodwill exists.

A well drafted partnership agreement will deal with goodwill. The majority of agreements state there is none. If goodwill is recognised there needs to be a way of valuing it and again a well drafted partnership agreement will cover how it is valued.

Where we are dealing with disputes and there is no agreement, then it is back to horse-trading. Goodwill is a partnership asset and needs to be protected.

Sometimes, as a final part of the negotiation, an ex-gratia payment may be made to an exiting partner. It can be termed goodwill. The reason is that a prolonged fight takes time and costs money and prevents the continuing partners from getting on and running the firm. It may be worth paying a premium to get the matter resolved quickly and so a premium is often offered to sweeten the exit. The exact sum will depend on the size of the overall payment offered and the cash flow of the firm.

Valuation

There are, in simple terms, two ways of valuing a business: one is the net assets from the last accounts and the other is a multiple of maintainable profits. If the multiple valuation exceeds the net asset value, the difference is goodwill. Let's consider an example – a firm with two partners has a net asset valuation of £750,000 and its past three years profits are as follows:

2021	2020	2019
£500,000	£450,000	£475,000

We can then weight the current year as 3, the penultimate year as 2 and the earliest year as 1 and divide the total by 6 to get a figure for weighted average maintainable profits. We get (500 x 3) + (450 x 2) + (475 x 1) all divided by 6 (3 + 2 + 1).

That is (1500 + 900 + 475) ÷ 6, which is 2,875 ÷ 6, which gives us £479,166 weighted average profits. for the past three years. You do not need to weight the profits and can consider including an estimate for the current year.

We need to consider any unusual items to be deducted or added back for any of the profits, for example a windfall payment or one-off expense. That would be added or deducted from the top number. If for the example the 2020 figures included a one-off £20,000 relocation expense, that should be added back in, making a top line profit figure of £470,000 and increasing the weighted average three-year profit to £485,833.

The next adjustment to make is that of a salary for the partners. We'll assume that it would cost £100,000 p.a. fully loaded

(National Insurance, pension, etc) to recruit an experienced person to do the job of each partner, assuming they were working in the business. We'll therefor deduct £200,000 from the maintainable earnings, giving a weighted average maintainable earnings figure for the business of £285,833. We'll use a rounded figure of £285,000.

Then a multiplier must be applied to the adjusted average weighted maintainable earnings figure. This will depend on the sector of the business. In general terms multipliers range from about three to eight. Hi-tec businesses or businesses where profits are easily maintained without the input of the owners are at the higher end. You will need to do some research into this. Beware of using the multiples applied to listed firms as these will be higher – we have seen issues in the legal sector recently where listed firms are showing way higher multiples than we are seeing in the market for unlisted firms.

The multiplier can be a source of disagreement between the parties and often an independent expert is appointed. Sometimes the parties appoint their own experts and there can be a difference of opinion as to the value. This the comes down to negotiation!

One recent case we acted on saw a director in a limited company professional "partnership" submit a large employment claim for unfair dismissal. This was successfully rebuffed but we were then able to argue that their shares must be worth significantly less because of the claim against the company, which if successful would significancy dent its profitability for the year, and eat into reserves.

Some businesses are valued on multiples of turnover rather than profit, primarily where that number is reasonably constant – one example of this is accountancy practices, where they are often valued around one times turnover.

You need to do your research on what similar businesses are worth.

When will the agreed sum be paid?

The next crucial element in the negotiations is when the payments will be made. The old adage is that cash now is always better than cash in the future and the more mathematical minded can calculate the exact value using discounted cash flow calculations.

At the time of writing interest rates are very low and so in cash terms this may be less important. £50,000 paid now at 0.5% interest is worth £50,250 in a year's time.

However, the parties will be balancing risk versus cash flow. For the departing partner, they may not trust their former partners to pay them when due (and then experience more prolonged and expensive legal wrangling) but the firm may not be able to afford to pay out the agreed settlement all at once or may not be able to borrow to pay it out. In the days of cheap borrowing, it can be a good negotiation tool to offer a discount to pay a settlement all in one go.

Another fear for a departing partner is that the firm does not survive for two or three years (or whatever the agreed payout period is) and they do not get the money. With a partnership the partners will be jointly and severally liable, but may not be good for the money and in an LLP a former partner owed money will just be another unsecured creditor, unless security is taken. Firms are always reluctant to give a departing partner security over the firm's assets, and other lenders may not allow it.

Negotiating security on deferred payments can be a tricky issue, but can be important for a departing partner.

How will leaving accounts prepared?

As discussed above, the preparation of the leaving accounts can be a contentious matter. The fear for the leaving partner is that the firm both depresses profits and increases costs to reduce their share of profits in their final year. On the other hand, the firm will not want a poorly performing, or poorly behaving, partner to reap the benefits of windfall or extra-ordinary profits that may have had no part in generating.

Even more contentious is where the firm feels that a departing partner should bear the brunt of losses that he or she has been personally liable for creating, for example where their negligence has resulted in a large claim against the firm. The standard position is that partners share profits and losses as agreed and that particular costs are not put against a specific partner. However, some Partnership or LLP Agreements do allow for the costs of negligent actions to be debited against a partner's capital or current accounts. This is unusual, but not unknown. Do check the agreement, but if there is no specific agreement to this, then it is not possible – other than by negotiation – to deduct the costs of a negligent action from a departing partner's profit share.

However, where the negligent action has reduced the value of the firm and the partner is looking for payment for his or her goodwill, it is perfectly fair to argue that the goodwill is reduced because of the reduction in the value of the firm.

Given the above, it is important that any Deed of Retirement contains clear guidance as to how the leaving accounts are to be prepared. It will usually require the accounts to be prepared on the same basis as previous years. This can still be open to manipulation if large billing is deferred until after year end, large expenditure is brought forward, or write-offs and depreciation are charged at higher rates. I have seen a firm attempt to bring forward dilapidations on its lease.

The Deed of Retirement should include a clause where an independent accountant is appointed to decide any areas of dispute.

What indemnities will be required either way?

It is not usual for a departing partner to give any indemnities to the firm, although I have seen them. It may be appropriate where the departing partner has done something negligent that may impact on the firm after his or her leaving date.

Most partnership of LLP Agreements indemnify the departing partner for losses after their leaving date and these are repeated in any Deed of Retirement.

This should not be contentious, except in very rare circumstances where there are specific issues to be addressed.

Will restrictive covenants be enforced, or will there be derogations?

This, as briefly covered above, is often one of the key negotiation areas for a settlement.

Do not confuse restrictive covenants against employees with restrictive covenants against partners; they are different and the courts will interpret them differently, often allowing much more restrictive covenants against a departing partner than against an employee (but not as much as against a selling partner in the event of a third-party sale).

The starting point to consider is how much use are the restrictive covenants in any event? This will depend on the sector and the specific firm.

If you have a trading firm (note: you really should consider incorporating it into a limited company!) the customer lists may be vital, especially in a customer facing role and absolutely in a selling role and you will therefore want to enforce the restrictive covenants as much as possible.

They key thing to contemplate is whether the customers are loyal to the individual or the firm. If the individual, there may be little that can be done to stop them going, although a well drafted covenant may make it difficult for the departing partner's new firm (or employer) to trade with those restricted customers.

You can write (or get your solicitor to write) to the departing partner's new firm or employer with a copy of the restrictive covenants pointing out that you may include them in any legal action, such as for inducing the departing partner to breach his or her covenants. Only make that threat if you are prepared to go through with it – and are willing to invest the time, energy and money to do so. It is a useful threat on occasions.

If you actually do enforce a restrictive covenant, it is not just the departing partner and the firm he or she is moving to who know it;

it is the other partners and senior staff who know that the firm is serious about protecting its goodwill. This can be an advantage in itself and acts as a warning to others who may be contemplating leaving and taking clients or customers with them.

When we are looking at professional firms, it is often more difficult to enforce the covenants. The Solicitors Regulation Authority in England and Wales is clear that clients must be free to instruct the firm of their choice.

If you tell a professional client that he, she (or even it) can't follow a departing partner to their new firm, what is the likelihood that they will stay with you in any event? They are likely to be upset and look around for a new provider of professional services. It sometimes makes sense to allow a departing partner to take some of the work if the client instructs you in other areas. If, in a law firm for example, a corporate partner leaves, you may retain property or employment work if there are strong relationships there. If you say that client that it can't instruct the corporate partner at their new firm, you may lose all the work in any event.

You also need to consider whether you have the staff and the skill sets to service the client when the departing partner leaves or whether it is an opportunity to review what you do.

The law does not like restrictive covenants, as they restrict business, but tolerates them if money has changed hands. The question judges will ask is along the lines of how long is necessary to allow the firm to put someone new in place to rebuild the customer or client relationships?

Our experience is that most Deeds of Retirement include the names of some clients that the departing partner will take with him or her.

They may be personal friends or family, but are more often clients that who only instruct that person and not the firm. There's another book to be written in how to make clients sticky to the firm, and not the individual, but it's too late now.

Restrictive covenants and which ones to enforce is a key negotiation tool for the firm in a partnership exit. It may also be key to the departing partner if he or she needs those clients or customers in their new role.

What agreed statements will be made to staff, clients, the market?

This is another key area for negotiation.

If the partner is being expelled or compulsorily retired, it will be key for them that the firm issues a statement to the effect that it is an agreed parting of the ways, thanking them for their contribution and wishing them well for the future.

Even more important is to agree the wording of any reference to future employers or firms. This ensures that "no scores are settled" and that everyone knows what will be said. I have had matters where this has taken a lot of time and numerous drafts to come up with an agreed reference and/or statement.

If the partner is leaving to go to a new firm, the current firm will want to ensure that it paints the departure in as positive light as possible.

The settlement agreement will include what we politely refer to as the "no slagging off" clause. That is an agreement from both parties and the partners in the firm not to say anything disparaging about the other and not to allow or encourage others to do so. Where the disagreement is acrimonious, this is important.

The timing of announcements to staff and the market are also important and it is important to agree who tells the departing partner's staff about their exit and what message is conveyed.

What confidentiality will be applied about the departure?

Confidentiality is linked to the section above on announcements. What message is given to the market and others in the firm?

It is usual that the terms of any departure are confidential.

Remember that all partners have access to all records of the partnership (also members in an LLP) and will be able to see what has been agreed unless the Partnership of LLP Agreement contains a clause allowing a management team to take confidential advice without sharing it with all partners. This is also particularly useful when a management team or senior partner is taking advice about removing a partner. Any advice taken by the firm is available to all partners – including the one potentially being removed. If you do not have an agreement with a clause allowing management to take confidential advice, the other partners and members will need to take that advice personally and it cannot be paid for by the partnership of LLP and nor can the VAT be reclaimed.

It is useful, in bigger firms, to keep the terms confidential in case they form a precedent for future departures.

Kit – laptops, phones, cars. etc

Of potentially less importance, but sometimes relevant, is what office equipment the departing partner can take with him or her.

The physical phone is less important than the phone number. An individual's mobile number, if stored in clients' or contacts' mobiles is a huge marketing tool. If the departing partner arrived with the number, it may well be theirs; if it was issued to them by the firm, then the firm can argue to keep it. Paying the contract for a number of months after the leaving date is often a nice thing to throw in to sweeten a package.

The same logic applies to laptop computers. The issue is what is left on them. The firm needs to make sure than any confidential client data is removed from the laptop (or other devices) before they leave the firm's control. the cost of a new laptop is not significant for many, but may again sweeten a deal.

Where firms pay for cars, you will have to decide what happens. Will the departing partner take over any contract or buy the car from the firm, and at what price? Will the firm continue to pay for the car for a period of time?

One interesting thing to consider is social media. Who owns a departing partner's LinkedIn profile and Twitter account? If the firm has paid to set them up and to run them, they are potentially a firm's asset. LinkedIn accounts are personal and it would be challenging to ask a departing partner to delete all the contacts they made during their tenure at the firm. I have seen partnership agreements that argue this. Twitter accounts are more easily arguable as firm property and it is possible to negotiate as to who keeps them. I have done this.

In a social media age, this ties in with restrictive covenants, as it becomes easier for a partner to let previous clients know where he or she has moved to via LinkedIn or Twitter.

The same arguments will apply to Instagram, Tik Tok and whatever else becomes trendy between writing and publication.

Intellectual property – precedents, etc

The final area that is often relevant, especially in professional practices, is intellectual property.

If a lawyer has developed some precedents whilst a partner in a firm, these will (most probably) belong to the firm and it may be a negotiation point to allow the departing partner to take some of their precedents with them. This would equally apply to other intellectual property developed in any firm.

A partnership is formed when two or more people go into business together with a view to a profit (Section 1, Partnership Act 1890). This leads to numerous accidental partnerships. Someone starts a business and their friend subsequently comes to help them; they are not an employee and suddenly a partnership has been formed. It only comes to light when they inevitably fall out.

This issue is often seen in the courts with bands. A few people start jamming together for fun; they then play some gigs in a local pub. It grows and they become global megastars. They are a partnership, although they may not realise it. When the eventual split for musical differences arises, who owns the copyright on the songs? This short book is not designed to answer that questions and the courts have debated it at length.

The point is that intellectual property is key to certain partnerships and when a partner leaves it can be a key negotiating tool to let him or her take some of it with them.

Conclusion

The aim of this chapter is to help you see what elements of persuading a partner to go are negotiable. There are many levers that can be pulled and a range of options on things that either party can offer the other to help facilitate a deal.

The chapter on outcomes sets out the way that partnership disputes usually end and you will need to persuade the other side why they should settle. If the end result is known – for example that one partner will leave and be paid out – then it is easier to discuss what shape the deal looks like and which of the other areas, discussed above, are relevant.

You will always need to persuade the other party that litigation is not the answer and that they need to settle. You need to explain clearly why settling will get them a better result than litigating. A better result includes all the aspects discussed above – you should focus on time, money, reputation and the ability to get on with life without the time, expense, stress and uncertainty of litigation.

CHAPTER SIX

SETTLEMENT

The final chapter of his book is about the settlement.

Once you have worked out where your dispute is likely to go and have negotiated a settlement, you need to commit the terms of the settlement to writing. Never be tempted to miss this stage – remember you are probably dealing with difficult people!

In a limited company situation, you will need to deal with employment rights and shares, necessitating a settlement agreement and a share purchase agreement, or share buy-back agreement with all the necessary minutes, resolutions and Companies House forms.

For a partnership or LLLP you will need a Deed of Retirement. This is a document that sets out the terms of the agreement and ends the departing partner's involvement in the firm.

Key clauses in the agreement must reflect the issues discussed in previous chapters.

The key elements will be:

- Parties – all partners in a partnership and the departing member and the LLP in an LLP. An LLP Deed of Retirement may include the continuing members as partis in the Deed of Retirement if they are either guaranteeing any payments or agreeing not to denigrate the departing partner.

- The leaving date – when they cease to be a partner. This ties in to when they cease to be entitled to any share of the profits of the firm.

- Agreement that all the partner's interest in the firm is cancelled on the leaving date and reverts to the other partners. There may be internal discussions on how they are distributed.

- The sums due to them for current account, capital account, tax account, goodwill and anything else – all clearly defined and specified.

- When each of the above sums will be paid; they can and usually are different. Profit share is usually paid sooner than capital or goodwill and tax is paid to the tax authorities when it is due.

- If there are deferred payments, is interest due on them and at what rate? What happens if a payment is missed or delayed? This usually results in increased interest and sometimes all sums become due immediately.

- Is security required for any deferred payments? On what and by whom?

- How the leaving accounts will be calculated and who the expert is to agree any disputes about them.

- Indemnities. It is usual to indemnify the outgoing partner for any liabilities after the leaving date.

- A restatement of the restrictive covenants (if in the agreement) or a new set and linked to a list of exceptions.

- A list of equipment and other property the partner can take with them.

- Agreed statements and references.

- Any variations to the main agreement going forward in terms of profit shares or capital.

- An arbitration clause in the event of disputes – you don't want litigation about the Deed of Retirement.

- Usual signing clauses.

The above list is not a precedent for a Deed of Retirement, nor is it comprehensive for every agreement, but us designed to help you focus on the key elements, which have been discussed in this short overview of partnership disputes.

In a partnership, it is in the outgoing partner's interest to have a notice placed in the London Gazette and a local newspaper near where the firm trades stating that he or she is no longer a partner as that prevents claims against them for periods after they ceased to be a partner.

In an LLP and a limited company, the appropriate form must be sent to Companies House and internal registers updated.

MORE BOOKS BY
LAW BRIEF PUBLISHING

A selection of our other titles available now:-

'A Practical Guide to Solicitor and Client Costs – 2nd Edition' by Robin Dunne

'Constructive Dismissal – Practice Pointers and Principles' by Benjimin Burgher

'A Practical Guide to Religion and Belief Discrimination Claims in the Workplace' by Kashif Ali

'A Practical Guide to the Law of Medical Treatment Decisions' by Ben Troke

'Fundamental Dishonesty and QOCS in Personal Injury Proceedings: Law and Practice' by Jake Rowley

'A Practical Guide to the Law in Relation to School Exclusions' by Charlotte Hadfield & Alice de Coverley

'A Practical Guide to Divorce for the Silver Separators' by Karin Walker

'The Right to be Forgotten – The Law and Practical Issues' by Melissa Stock

'A Practical Guide to Planning Law and Rights of Way in National Parks, the Broads and AONBs' by James Maurici QC, James Neill et al

'A Practical Guide to Election Law' by Tom Tabori

'A Practical Guide to the Law in Relation to Surrogacy' by Andrew Powell

'A Practical Guide to Claims Arising from Fatal Accidents – 2nd Edition' by James Patience

'A Practical Guide to the Ownership of Employee Inventions – From Entitlement to Compensation' by James Tumbridge & Ashley Roughton

'A Practical Guide to Asbestos Claims' by Jonathan Owen & Gareth McAloon

'A Practical Guide to Stamp Duty Land Tax in England and Northern Ireland' by Suzanne O'Hara

'A Practical Guide to the Law of Farming Partnerships' by Philip Whitcomb

'A Practical Guide to Financial Ombudsman Service Claims'
by Adam Temple & Robert Scrivenor

'A Practical Guide to Advising Schools on Employment Law' by Jonathan Holden

'A Practical Guide to Running Housing Disrepair and Cavity Wall Claims:
2nd Edition' by Andrew Mckie & Ian Skeate

'A Practical Guide to Holiday Sickness Claims – 2nd Edition'
by Andrew Mckie & Ian Skeate

'Arguments and Tactics for Personal Injury and Clinical Negligence Claims'
by Dorian Williams

'A Practical Guide to Drone Law' by Rufus Ballaster, Andrew Firman, Eleanor Clot

'A Practical Guide to Compliance for Personal Injury Firms Working With Claims
Management Companies' by Paul Bennett

'A Practical Guide to Dog Law for Owners and Others' by Andrea Pitt

'RTA Allegations of Fraud in a Post-Jackson Era: The Handbook – 2nd Edition'
by Andrew Mckie

'RTA Personal Injury Claims: A Practical Guide Post-Jackson' by Andrew Mckie

'On Experts: CPR35 for Lawyers and Experts' by David Boyle

'An Introduction to Personal Injury Law' by David Boyle

'A Practical Guide to Subtle Brain Injury Claims' by Pankaj Madan

These books and more are available to order online direct from the publisher at www.lawbriefpublishing.com, where you can also read free sample chapters. For any queries, contact us on 0844 587 2383 or mail@lawbriefpublishing.com.

Our books are also usually in stock at www.amazon.co.uk with free next day delivery for Prime members, and at good legal bookshops such as Wildy & Sons.

We are regularly launching new books in our series of practical day-to-day practitioners' guides. Visit our website and join our free newsletter to be kept informed and to receive special offers, free chapters, etc.

You can also follow us on Twitter at www.twitter.com/lawbriefpub.